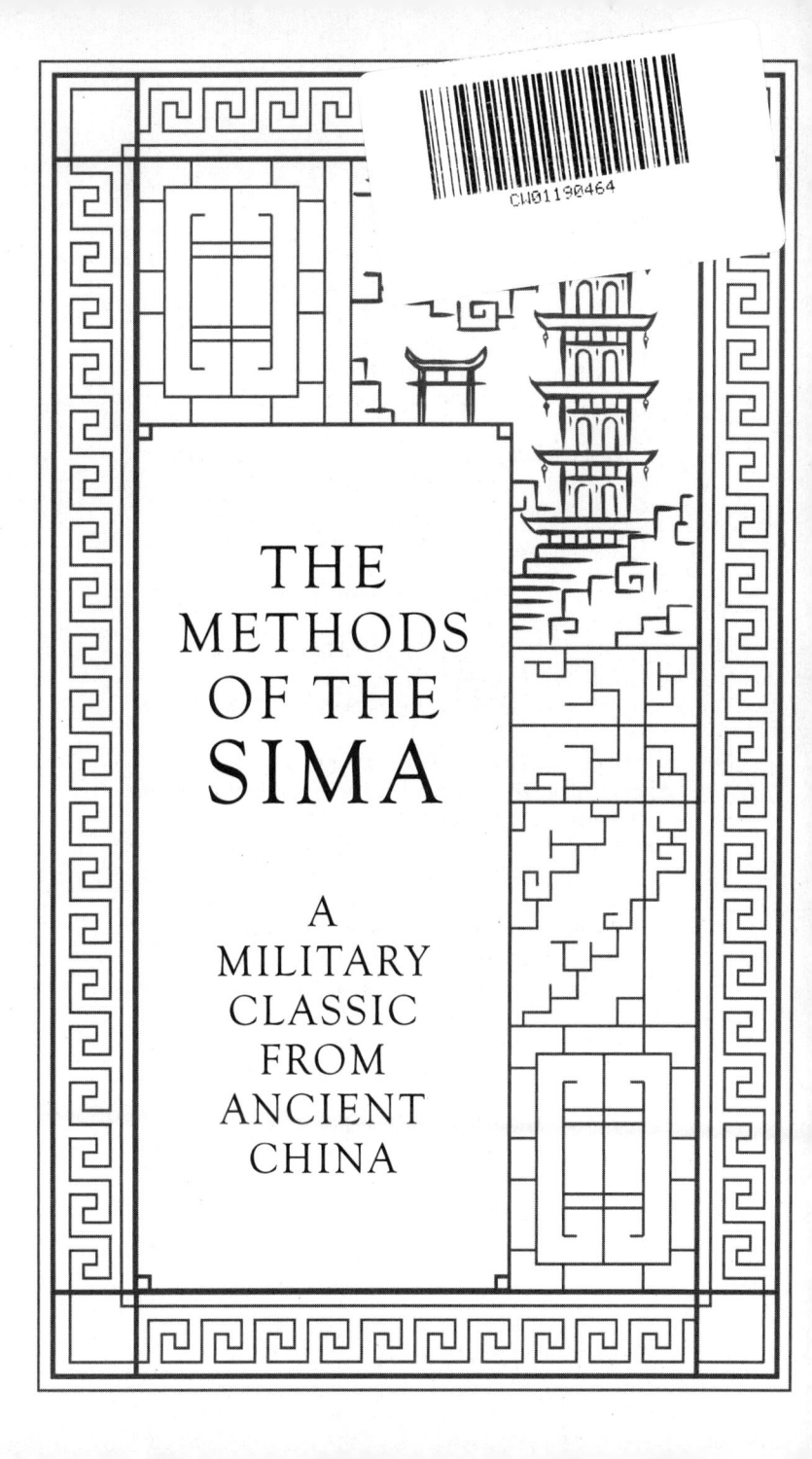

THE METHODS OF THE SIMA

A MILITARY CLASSIC FROM ANCIENT CHINA

Cherry Stone Publishing, an imprint of
Sweet Cherry Publishing Limited
Unit 36, Vulcan House,
Vulcan Road,
Leicester, LE5 3EF
United Kingdom

First published by Cherry Stone Publishing in 2021
2021 edition

2 4 6 8 10 9 7 5 3 1

ISBN: 978-1-78226-963-2

© Sweet Cherry Publishing

The Methods of the Sima

All rights reserved. No part of this publication may be
reproduced or utilised in any form or by any means, electronic
or mechanical, including photocopying, recording, or using
any information storage and retrieval system, without prior
permission in writing from the publisher.

This book is copyright under the Berne Convention.
No reproduction without permission.
All rights reserved.

Cover design and illustrations
by Sophie Jones

www.cherrystonepublishing.com

Printed and bound in India
I.TP002

THE METHODS OF THE SIMA

ANCIENT PRINCIPLES AND METHODS OF WARFARE

CHERRY STONE PUBLISHING

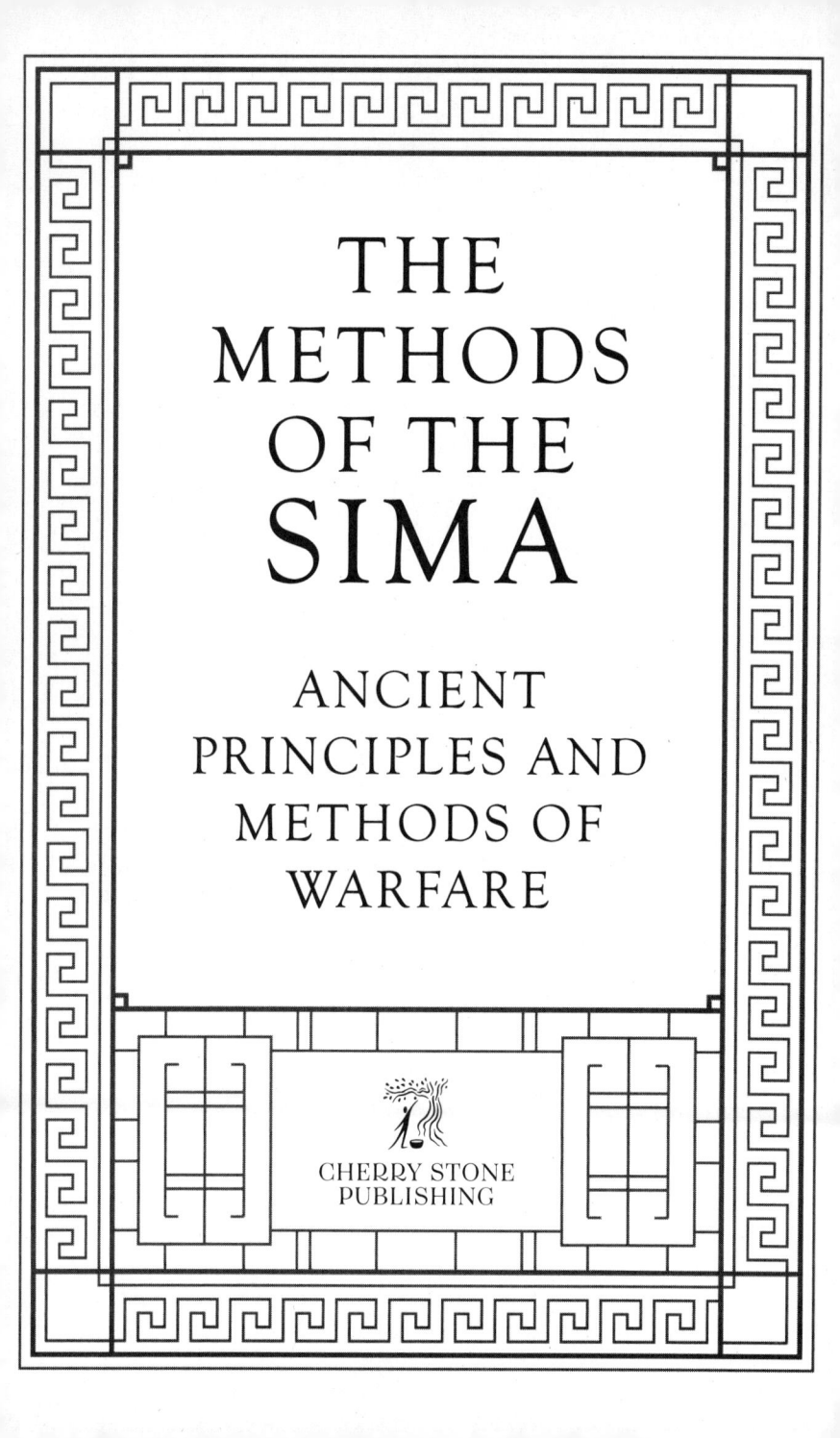

CHAPTER I.

BENEVOLENCE

THE METHODS OF THE SIMA

1

In antiquity, taking benevolence as the foundation and employing righteousness constituted governance.

2

However, when governance fails to attain the desired moral and political objectives, it is essential to resort to authority. Authority comes from warfare, not from the harmony among people.

3

For this reason, if one must kill to bring peace to the people, then killing is permissible.

4

If one must attack a state out of the love for the people, then attacking is permissible.

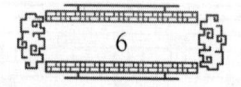

BENEVOLENCE

5

If one must stop war with war, although it is war, it is permissible.

6

Thus, if a ruler shows benevolence, he will be loved; if a ruler shows righteousness, he will be willingly submitted to; if a ruler shows wisdom, he will be relied upon; if a ruler shows courage, he will be embraced; if a ruler shows integrity, he will be trusted.

7

In this way, he will be loved by the people internally, so that he can defend his country; externally, he will be a deterrent, so that he can defeat his enemies.

8

The way of warfare is neither contravening the seasons nor working the people to exhaustion.

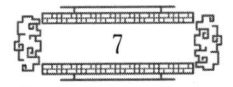

THE METHODS OF THE SIMA

9

Cruelty is no means by which to love the people.

10

Neither attacking a state in national mourning, nor taking advantage of natural disaster is the means by which to attack an enemy state.

11

Not mobilizing the army in either winter or summer is the means by which to love both your own people and the enemy's people, as you should not put people through these harsh conditions unless absolutely necessary.

12

Even though a state may be vast, if it is belligerent, it will inevitably perish.

BENEVOLENCE

13

Even though calm may prevail in the realm, those who forget warfare will certainly be endangered, which is no way to love the people at all.

14

So if you love your people, you must not let them forget about the necessity for war.

15

Even when all under Heaven is peaceful and happy, one must still use hunting trips as war exercises and one must still train the army during spring and summer.

16

This is to make sure that the preparations of war are not forgotten.

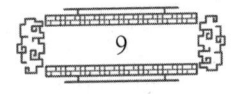

THE METHODS OF THE SIMA

17

In antiquity, it was a sign of courtesy not to chase a fleeing enemy more than one hundred steps and not to follow a retreating enemy more than ninety *li**.

18

It was a sign of benevolence not to kill an enemy incapacitated and to pity its sick and wounded.

19

It was a sign of good faith to wait for the enemy to finish setting up before attacking.

20

It was a sign of the justice of war to fight for the greater good and not for the lesser.

---

*li is a traditional Chinese unit of distance that is about a half-kilometre long.

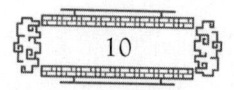

BENEVOLENCE

21

It was a sign of courage to pardon a surrendered enemy.

22

It was the sign of wisdom to foresee the beginning and end of war.

23

These six virtues were taught to the population at proper times and served as a code of conduct for the masses as well as the method of managing the army since ancient times.

24

The administrative measures of the former kings were in line with the Way of the Heaven.

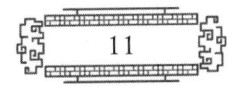

THE METHODS OF THE SIMA

25

They would establish commanders and leaders at places where they were most beneficial. They prioritised placing the virtuous in the office.

26

Ranks were exalted due to the amount of virtue a commander was able to wield.

27

In the days of former kings and feudal lords only the virtuous could ever reign.

28

Foreign states also came to submit before the ultimately virtuous state, where punishment and war ceased. This type of leadership is known as the sage rule.

BENEVOLENCE

29

What is more, wise kings ordered the rites, music, laws and measures and then set up the five punishments, and raised armoured troops to crush injustice.

30

They made inspection tours of the feudal lands, assembled the feudal lords, and investigated differences.

31

If any of the feudal lords had disobeyed orders, broken laws, corrupted morals, contravened the seasons of Heaven, or endangered meritorious officers, the rulers would make it well known among the feudal lords, making it evident that offences were committed.

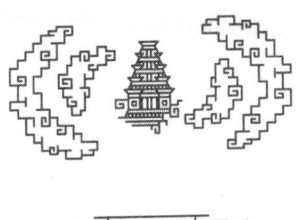

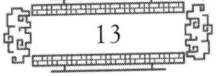

THE METHODS OF THE SIMA

32

Then the rulers would hold rituals of praying to Heaven and Earth for ancestors, to the gods of the land, the four directions, the mountains and rivers and to the local sites of social worship.

33

Then they offered sacrifice to the former kings.

34

Only thereafter would the prime ministers charge the army before the feudal lords, saying, "A certain state has acted contrary to the Way. You will participate in a rectification campaign on a certain date. On that date, the army will reach the offending state and assemble with the Son of Heaven to apply the punishment of rectification."

BENEVOLENCE

35

The prime ministers and other high officials would issue the following orders to the army: "When you enter the offender's territory, you are forbidden to desecrate the gods, hunt, destroy waterworks, burn houses and buildings, cut down trees, or take livestock, food and utensils without permission. When you see their elderly or very young, return them without harming them. Even if you encounter adults, unless they engage you in combat, do not treat them as enemies. If an enemy has been wounded, provide medical attention and return him."

36

When the guilty had been executed, the rulers, together with the feudal lords, corrected and rectified the government and customs of the state.

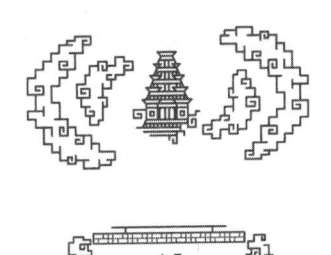

THE METHODS OF THE SIMA

37

They promoted the worthy, established an enlightened ruler and corrected and restored their feudal positions and obligations.

38

The ways by which the kings and the hegemons governed the feudal lords were six: to control the lords by adjusting the size of their fiefs; to restrain them by policy and decree; to keep them close with courtesy and prestige; to please them with gifts of wealth; to support them with wise and resourceful men; and to intimidate them with a powerful army.

39

By sharing weals and woes with the lords, the kings united them, bringing harmony between smaller and larger states.

BENEVOLENCE

40

The kings and hegemons assembled the feudal lords in order to announce nine prohibitions.

41

Those who took advantage of the weak states or encroached them shall have their borders reduced.

42

Those who murdered the worthy or harmed the people shall be deposed.

43

Those who were brutal within their states and bullied weaker states shall be purged.

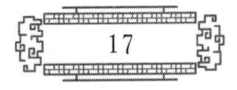

THE METHODS OF THE SIMA

44

Those who caused the field to be desolate and the people to scatter shall be reduced.

45

Those who relied on their terrain advantage and refused to submit shall be invaded. Those who harmed or killed his kinsmen shall be punished.

46

Those who deposed or killed their rulers shall be exterminated. Those who opposed orders and resisted the government shall be squashed.

47

Those who committed internal or external debauchery, and behaved like a beast shall be extinguished.

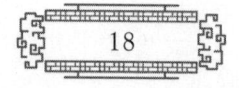

CHAPTER II.

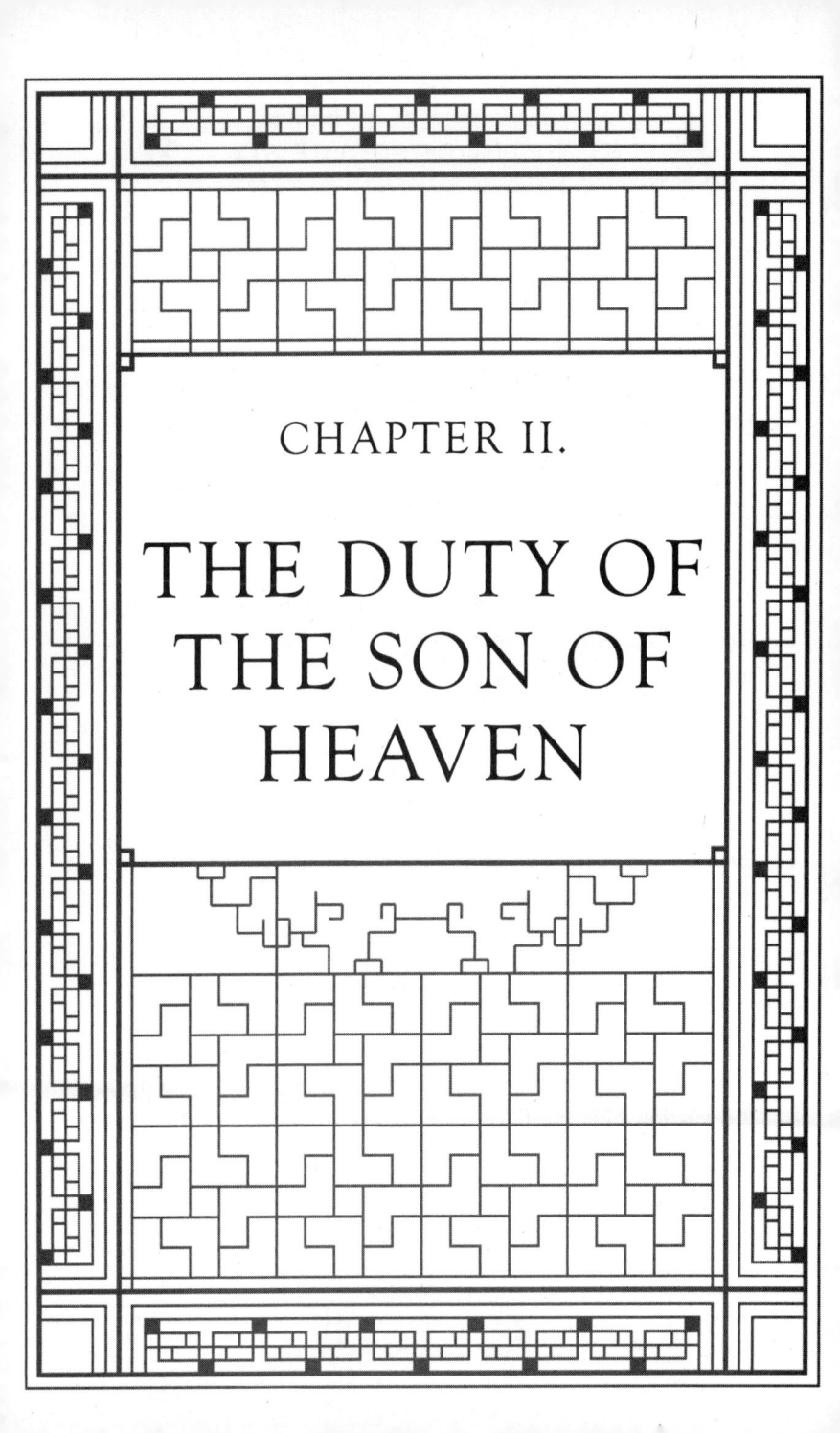

THE DUTY OF THE SON OF HEAVEN

THE METHODS OF THE SIMA

1

The duty of the Son of Heaven is to take the teachings of Heaven and Earth and to learn from the ancient saints and kings.

2

The duty of officers and common men must be to respectfully serve their parents and to be upright with their rulers and superiors.

3

Even though there is an enlightened ruler, if the officers are not first instructed, they cannot be used.

4

When the ancients instructed the people, they would establish the relationships and fixed distinctions of noble and common so that the people did not encroach on each other.

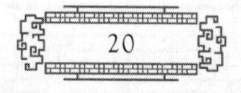

THE DUTY OF THE SON OF HEAVEN

5

The virtuous and righteous did not exceed each other; the talented and technically skilled could be used; and the courageous and strong did not clash with authority.

6

Thus, their strength would be united and their thoughts in harmony.

7

In antiquity, the rules governing the state could not be used in military; and those appropriate in the military may not be appropriate in governing the state.

8

Thus, righteousness and virtue did not infringe each other.

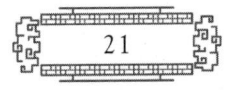

THE METHODS OF THE SIMA

9

The ruler must honour those who do not boast, for those who do not boast are precious talents to the ruler; if he can refrain from boasting, it means that he has no extravagant expectations, and if he has no extravagant expectations, he will not compete with others.

10

When the ruler seeks opinions from these people, he will certainly grasp the true situation, and if the army listens to these people, things will be handled properly, so that those with talent and skill will not be buried.

11

For those that follow orders, they should be rewarded well; for those that defy orders, they should be severely punished.

12

Then the strong and courageous will not clash with authority.

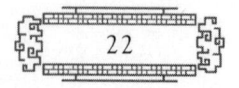

THE DUTY OF THE SON OF HEAVEN

13

Only after effective instructions have been given to the people, can the state carefully select and employ them.

14

When government affairs are thoroughly managed, officers are able to do their duty.

15

When the content of education is simple and concise, the people will easily learn it well, and once habits are formed, the people will act according to custom.

16

This is the greatest effectiveness of education.

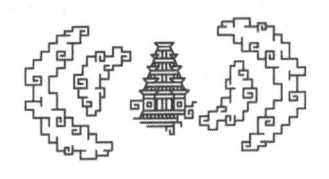

THE METHODS OF THE SIMA

17

In antiquity, the army used to chase a fleeing enemy without going too far, and to track an enemy who retreated of his own accord without coming too close.

18

By not pursuing too far, the army would not be lured; by not pursuing too closely, it would not be ambushed.

19

By using propriety as the norm, the army will be consolidated, and by using benevolence as the aim, the enemy will be overcome.

20

With this method, after victory, it could be used again and again, and thus the virtuous valued this method.

THE DUTY OF THE SON OF HEAVEN

21

The You Yu Family admonished the people at home in order that they might understand his commands.

22

The rulers of the Xia Dynasty administered their oaths in the army for they wanted their people to be mentally prepared.

23

The rulers of the Yin Dynasty swore their oaths outside the military camp, for they wanted the people to understand the intentions first before going into battle.

24

The rulers of the Zhou Dynasty made the oath just before the two armies clashed, in order to stimulate the people's will to fight.

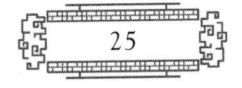

THE METHODS OF THE SIMA

25

The rulers of Xia acted in accordance to their virtues and never employed weapons, so their weapons were ralatively simple.

26

The rulers of Yin relied on righteousness, so they first used weapons.

27

The rulers of Zhou relied on force, so they invented and fully utilised all kinds of weapons.

28

In the Xia Dynasty, the rulers rewarded meritorious people at court to encourage virtues.

THE DUTY OF THE SON OF HEAVEN

29

In the Yin Dynasty, the rulers carried out executions in the marketplace to warn the evil.

30

In the Zhou Dynasty, the rulers granted rewards in court and carried out execution in the marketplace to promote virtues and terrify the non-gentleman.

31

Thus, although the methods differed, the rulers of all three dynasties aimed to manifest virtues.

32

Weapons cannot be effective unless they are used in conjunction with each other.

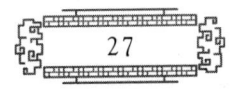

THE METHODS OF THE SIMA

33

Long weapons are for protection. Short weapons are for defence.

34

If the weapons are too long, they will be difficult to wield against others; If they are too short, they cannot reach the enemy.

35

If they are too light, they are fragile, and if they are fragile, they will break easily.

36

If they are too heavy, they will not be sharp and will never attain its objectives.

THE DUTY OF THE SON OF HEAVEN

37

War Chariots: Those from the Xia Dynasty were called "Hook Chariots", and their advantage was smooth-riding.

38

Those from the Yin Dynasty were called "Yin Chariots" and their advantage was speed.

39

Those from the Zhou Dynasty were called "Yuan Rong" and their advantage was the structural strength.

40

Flags: The Xia Dynasty used a black one, representing the majesty like holding a human head.

THE METHODS OF THE SIMA

41

The Yin's was white, representing the righteousness of Heaven.

42

The Zhou's was yellow, representing the Way of the Earth.

43

Emblem: The Xia used the sun and the moon to signify brightness. The Yin used tiger to indicate majesty. The Zhou used dragon to honour culture.

44

If the army is ruled with too much authority, the morale of the soldiers will be suppressed, and lacking in prestige, it will be difficult to command the soldiers to overcome the enemy.

THE DUTY OF THE SON OF HEAVEN

45

If superiors use the people's power inappropriately, if they appoint officials inappropriately, if a skilled person is unable to fulfil his role, and if cattle and horses are not used wisely, and if those in charge are overbearing in forcing people to obey, then excessive authority takes place.

46

And the people will cower as a result.

47

If superiors do not respect virtues but employ the deceptive and evil, if they do not honour those that follow the Way but employ those that are tyrannical, if they do not value those who obey commands but instead esteem those that contravene them and if they do not value good actions but esteem violent behaviour, then diminished authority takes place.

THE METHODS OF THE SIMA

48

And the people will not be victorious as a result.

49

The army should move with calmness and unhurriedness, and calmness and unhurriedness will keep the soldiers' strength sufficient.

50

Then even when the blades clash, the infantry will not run and chariots will not gallop.

51

When pursuing a fleeing army, the troops will not break formation, thereby avoiding chaos.

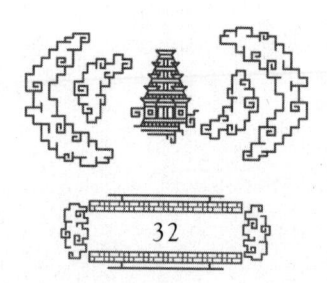

THE DUTY OF THE SON OF HEAVEN

52

The solidarity of the army derives from military discipline that maintains order in formation, does not exhaust the strength of men or horses and does not exceed the measures of the commands whether moving slowly or rapidly.

53

In antiquity, the form and spirit governing the ceremonial laws would not be found in the military realm; those appropriate to the military realm would not be found in the ceremonial laws.

54

If the form and spirit appropriate to the military realm entered the ceremonial law, the virtues of the people would decline.

55

When the form and spirit appropriate to ceremonial law entered the military realm, then the martial spirit of the troop would weaken.

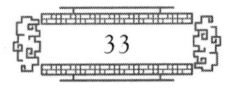

THE METHODS OF THE SIMA

56

For in the court, one should speak with gentleness and elegance, be respectful and humble in one's attitude when meeting the sovereign, be strict with oneself and lenient with others, not come without being summoned by the king, not speak without being asked, be grand in courtesy when meeting, but simple in resignation.

57

They should not kneel in armour, nor salute in chariots, nor walk in haste in the city, so as not to disturb the soldiers, nor be afraid of danger, so as not to confuse the army.

58

So ritual and law are used in conjunction with each other, and civil and military matters are not to be neglected.

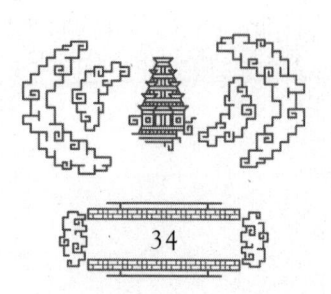

THE DUTY OF THE SON OF HEAVEN

59

In antiquity, the wise kings made manifest the virtues of the people and fully sought out the goodness of people. Thus they did not neglect the virtuous nor demean the people in any respect.

60

Rewards were not granted, punishment were never even tried.

61

The You Yu Family neither granted rewards not imposed punishments, but the people could still be employed. This was the height of virtues.

62

The Xia granted rewards but did not impose punishment. This was the height of instruction. The Yin imposed punishment but did not grant rewards. This was the height of awe. The Zhou used both rewards and punishment, causing virtues to decline.

THE METHODS OF THE SIMA

63

Rewards should not be delayed beyond the appropriate time for the people are supposed to quickly reap the benefits of good deeds.

64

Punishments should be carried out on the spot, so that the people would quickly see the evil consequences of evil-doing.

65

Do not reward great victories, for then neither the upper nor lower ranks will boast of their achievement.

66

If the upper ranks cannot boast, they will not seem arrogant, while if the lower ranks cannot boast, they will not compare themselves with the superiors.

THE DUTY OF THE SON OF HEAVEN

67

It is the pinnacle of humility for both the top and the bottom to refrain from boasting in this way.

68

In cases of great defeat, do not punish anyone, for then the upper and lower ranks will assume the disgrace falls on them.

69

If the upper ranks reproach themselves, they will certainly regret their errors; while if the lower ranks feel the same, they will certainly try to avoid repeating the offence.

70

It is also the pinnacle of humility for both superiors and subordinates to share the responsibility for their mistakes in this way.

THE METHODS OF THE SIMA

71

In antiquity, soldiers on the frontier were not required to serve labour duty for three years thereafter because they were already working too hard.

72

This was a sign of solidarity, and it was a sign of mutual compassion from above and below.

73

When a battle was won, a triumphant song was sung to express the joy of the occasion.

74

The Spirit Terrace was erected to celebrate the end of labour of the people and to show that time for rest had come.

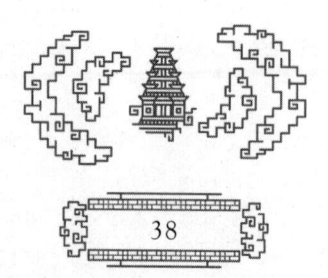

CHAPTER III.

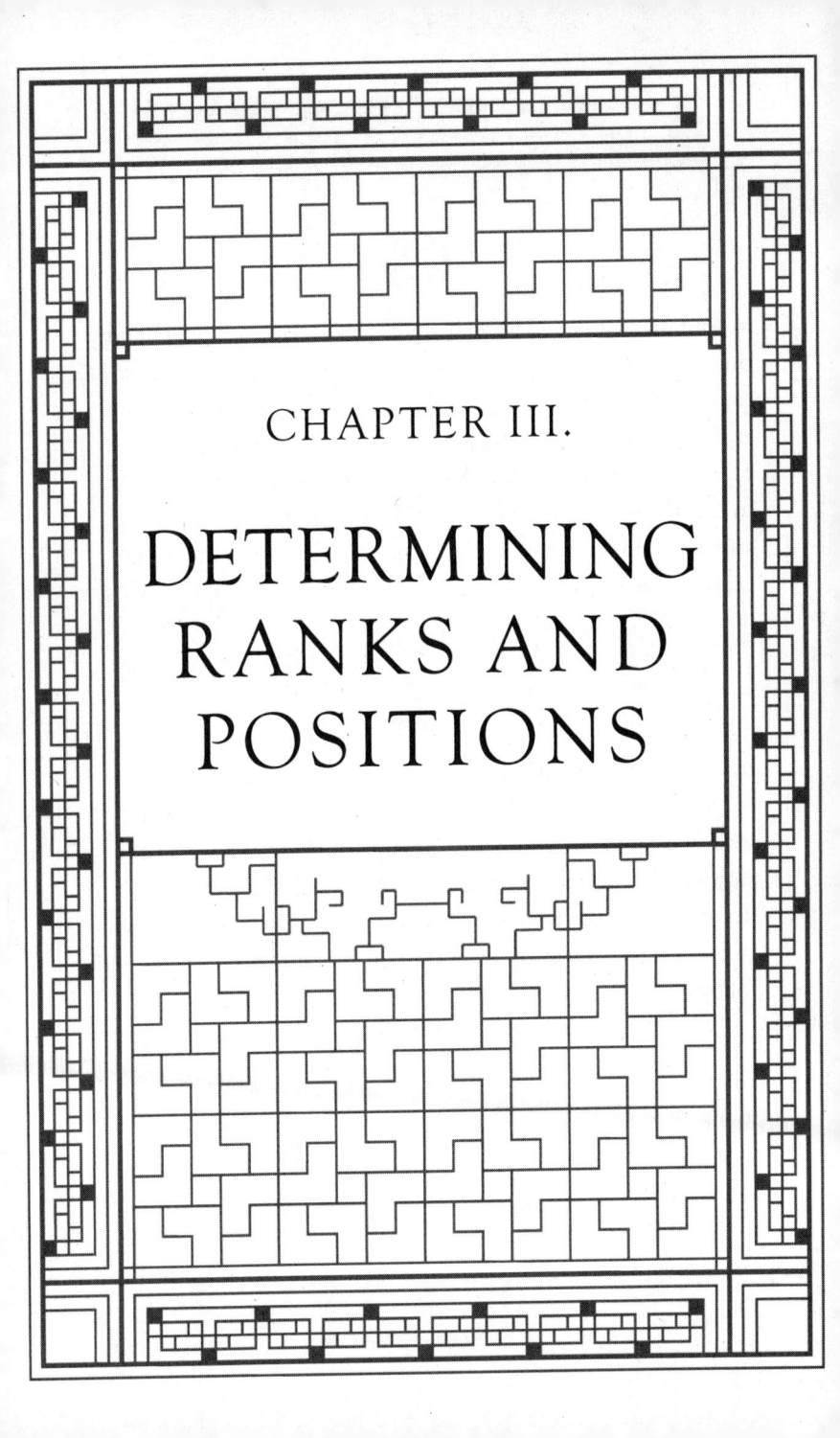

DETERMINING RANKS AND POSITIONS

THE METHODS OF THE SIMA

1

In warfare, it is necessary first to determine the rank and file of the army, to announce a system of rewards and punishments, to recruit soldiers from all walks of life, to give orders to the army, to consult the public, to recruit skilled men, to consider many aspects, to ascertain the root causes of various situations, to distinguish and inquire into difficult questions, to build up strength, to seek ingenious plans, and to act according to the wishes of the people.

2

In warfare, the following needs to be done: strengthen the hearts and minds of the army, distinguish what is good and what is bad, manage chaos, be disciplined in advancing and stopping, obey justice, inspire honesty and shame, simplify decrees, use fewer penalties, and stop small crimes; if those who commit small crimes succeed, those who commit big crimes will follow.

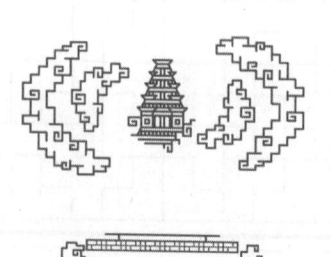

DETERMINING RANKS AND POSITIONS

3

These are the five things that must be considered in warfare: responding to the times of Heaven, collecting money, pleasing the hearts of the people, making use of the terrain, and paying attention to the use of weapons.

4

To follow the times of heaven means to make use of the seasons and to act in accordance with the times.

5

To gather wealth and resources means to make use of the enemy's supplies to strengthen our strength.

6

Convincing the hearts and minds of the people means responding to the will of the people to encourage the soldiers to kill the enemy.

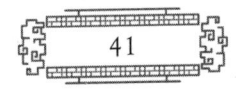

THE METHODS OF THE SIMA

7

To make use of the terrain means to control the defiles, dangers and obstructions.

8

To emphasise the use of weapons means to use bows and spears for cover, spears for defence and spears for assistance in battle.

9

Now each of these five weapons has its appropriate use: The long protects the short, the short rescues the long.

10

When they are used in turn, the battle can be sustained.

11

When they are employed all at once, the army will be strong.

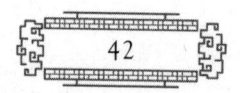

DETERMINING RANKS AND POSITIONS

12

If you find that the enemy uses a new weapon, you should follow suit in order to maintain a balance of power with the enemy.

13

The commanding general should be good at motivating his troops and boost their morale.

14

He also needs to monitor the changes in the enemy's camp and takes necessary precautions.

15

The minds of the troops and the general must be together as one.

16

Horses and oxen are well fed; chariots and weapons are maintained well: these are the strengths of the army.

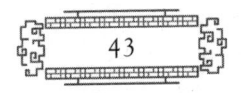

THE METHODS OF THE SIMA

17

Training should be done during peaceful times, as only then will there be order in the army during war.

18

The whole army is like a human, where the commanding general is the body, the soldiers are the arms and limbs, and the whole troops are the toes and fingers.

19

Warfare is a matter of wisdom. Combat is a matter of courage. The deployment of formations is a matter of skill.

20

You must strive to achieve your intentions, but you must also do what is within your power, and not do what is against your intentions or beyond your power.

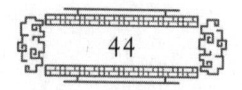

DETERMINING RANKS AND POSITIONS

21

With the enemy, on the contrary, they should be made to do what they are unwilling or unable to do.

22

In warfare, one must have Heaven, material resources and excellence.

23

When a good time comes, do not miss it, and when there is a sign of victory in divination, act confidentially.

24

This is the situation in which "having Heaven" takes place. When the masses are rich and plentiful and so is the state, this is the situation in which "having resources" takes place.

THE METHODS OF THE SIMA

25

When the army is well-trained, skilled in formation, and prepared with supplies and equipment, this is the situation in which "having excellence" takes place.

26

When the people are encouraged and give their best in fulfilling their responsibilities, they are "happy people".

27

Increasing the strength of the army and making the formations solid; making the numbers adequate and constantly training the troops; relying on the many talents to manage all military affairs; perceiving the nature of things and responding to the sudden events.

28

This is the situation when preparation for the foreseeable takes place.

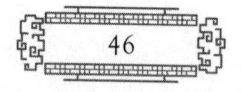

DETERMINING RANKS AND POSITIONS

29

Fast chariots and fleet infantrymen, bows and arrows, and a strong defence are what are needed for a powerful army.

30

The concentration of soldiers, the calmness of the army and the morale of the troops are what are needed for strengthening the formations.

31

On this basis, being able to advance or withdraw helps multiply army strength.

32

When the general is calm and the troops are well-drilled, that is good training.

THE METHODS OF THE SIMA

33

When there are appropriate offices, all matters are well managed.

34

When in accord with this, things are perceived and managed, therefore administration is streamlined.

35

Determine the size of your troops according to the terrain, and deploy your formation according to the enemy's situation.

36

When it is time to attack, wage battle, defend, advance, retreat and stop, the front and rear are ordered and the chariots and infantry move in concord; these are matters that need to be considered during war.

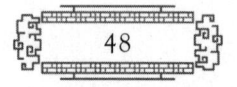

DETERMINING RANKS AND POSITIONS

37

Disobedience, distrust, disharmony, discord, neglect of duty, mutual suspicion, aversion to fighting, fear of the enemy, disorganization, mutual reproach, difficulty in redressing grievances, fatigue, recklessness, disintegration, lack of discipline – all these are the scourges of warfare.

38

When the army suffers from extreme arrogance, abject terror, moaning and grumbling, constant fear and show frequent regrets over actions taken, these will cause the demise of the army.

39

Being able to be large or small or firm or weak, to change formations, and to use large numbers or small groups with respect to the enemy's situation – all these contribute to the control of warfare.

THE METHODS OF THE SIMA

40

In warfare, the army should employ spies against the distant and observe the near, seize opportunities, take advantage of the enemy's material resources where possible, and esteem good faith and abhor the doubtful.

41

Arouse the soldiers with fervour of righteousness. Undertake affairs at the appropriate time. Employ people with kindness.

42

When you see the enemy, remain quiet; when you see turbulence, do not be hasty to respond; when you see danger and hardship, do not abandon the masses.

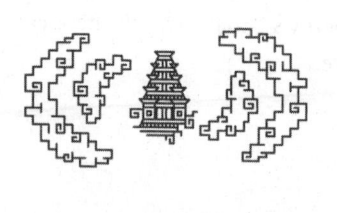

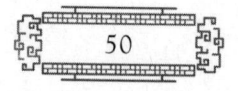

DETERMINING RANKS AND POSITIONS

43

Within the state, be generous and foster good faith. Within the army, be magnanimous but strict. When facing the enemy, be decisive and nimble.

44

Within the state, there should be harmony across all ranks. Within the army, rules must be clear and strictly adhered to. When facing the enemy, investigate the situation well.

45

Within the state, display virtues. Within the army, display uprightness. In warfare, display good faith.

46

In a general formation, the ranks of the army must be both spread out so that weapons can be densely arranged so that they can be used in battle.

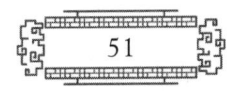

THE METHODS OF THE SIMA

47

Weapons must be used in a variety of ways, soldiers must be well-trained and calm, and the formation must be neat and tidy.

48

When orders are clear and accurate, the upper and lower ranks observe righteousness; only then will the troops be motivated.

49

When many well-conceived plans prove successful, the people will be convinced. When people are convinced, things can be done in order.

50

When the banners are bright and clear, then the troops can see it clearly. Once a battle plan has been determined, determination should be firm.

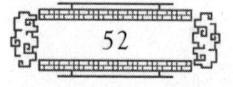

DETERMINING RANKS AND POSITIONS

51

Those who are indecisive and non-strategic in meeting the enemy should be punished.

52

Do not use the drums indiscriminately and do not change the banners easily as this may cause misunderstanding and confusion.

53

Whenever tasks are well-executed, they will endure; when they accord with ancient ways, they can be fulfilled successfully.

54

When the oath is clear, morale will be high and you can extinguish the enemy.

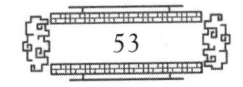

THE METHODS OF THE SIMA

55

The way to destroy the enemy: one is to use moral righteousness.

56

It is to convince the enemy with honesty, to deter them with might, to create a situation of unity, and to make people's hearts happy, and this will win the enemy's people to my use.

57

The second is to use power to make the enemy submit.

58

It is to seek to foster the enemy's arrogance, to seize the enemy's key points, to attack it from the outside with troops; and to spy on it from within.

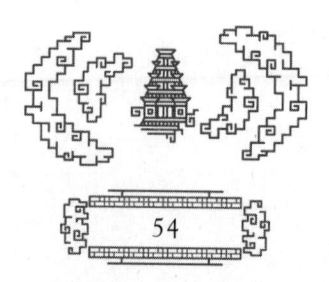

DETERMINING RANKS AND POSITIONS

59

First is management of talents; second is strict adherence to rules; third is clear orders and cause; fourth is management of skills; fifth is skill in using fire attacks; sixth is skill in water warfare; seventh is skill in using weapons.

60

These are referred to as the Seven Military Policies; Glory, profit, shame and death are referred to as the Four Controls that will make people observe the rules.

61

Reasoning in a pleasant manner or discipline in a severe manner is only to convert men to good. These are all military governance. Only benevolence can bring people closer.

62

But to speak of kindness without faith is to bring about defeat.

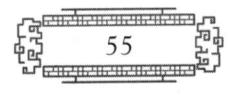

THE METHODS OF THE SIMA

63

To employ people, you must know the right people, correct yourself, employ the appropriate language, and use fire attacks only when necessary.

64

The principles of general warfare: having boosted morale, discipline must follow.

65

Treat your soldiers with kindness, and teach them with sincerity. Use their fear to warn them and their desire to control them.

66

Enter the enemy's territory to control favourable terrain, and assign the generals to their tasks according to their positions; this is the law of war.

DETERMINING RANKS AND POSITIONS

67

Protocols and policies of tasks and systems that are to be executed should come from the masses.

68

They should be tested and evaluated to the furthest extent.

69

If there is something that can be done but is not done, then the general should lead by example on how the tasks and system should be executed.

70

If everything is done, then make sure the troops know them.

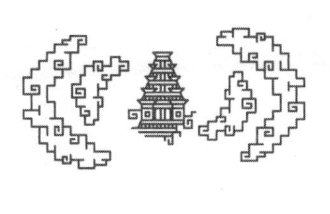

THE METHODS OF THE SIMA

71

By executing them several times, people will in time remember them and they become true protocols and policies.

72

And soon these protocols and policies would be known as the law.

73

The way to manage chaos or imposing order consists of benevolence, credibility, straightforwardness, unity, righteousness, change wrought by authority and centralised authority.

74

To establish the rule of law, one must be acceptable to the people; secondly, the decree must be clear; thirdly, the law must be followed; fourthly; it must be enforced with great speed; fifthly, the system of uniforms for all levels must be prescribed; sixthly, colours must be used to distinguish between ranks, and seventhly, officials must be dressed in accordance with the regulations and there must be no confusion.

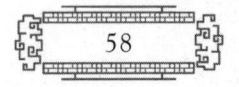

DETERMINING RANKS AND POSITIONS

75

In the case of the military, the authority is centralised if the execution of the decree is entirely in the hands of the general.

76

The law is truly established as the law only if it is observed by both above and below.

77

In the army, troops should not listen to commands from dubious sources.

78

When in battle, they should not hanker small advantages, their plans should achieve result successfully and should be executed in subtle fashion.

THE METHODS OF THE SIMA

79

In warfare, when normal methods do not prove to be effective, then centralised control must be undertaken; if people do not obey, then laws will have to be imposed.

80

If they do not trust each other, unite them. If they are dilatory, motivate them. If they have doubts, try to change them.

81

If people do not trust the orders of their superiors, the superiors should carry out firmly the orders and not change them easily.

82

These have been the methods of governing the army in combat since ancient times.

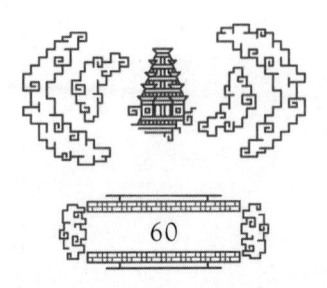

CHAPTER IV.

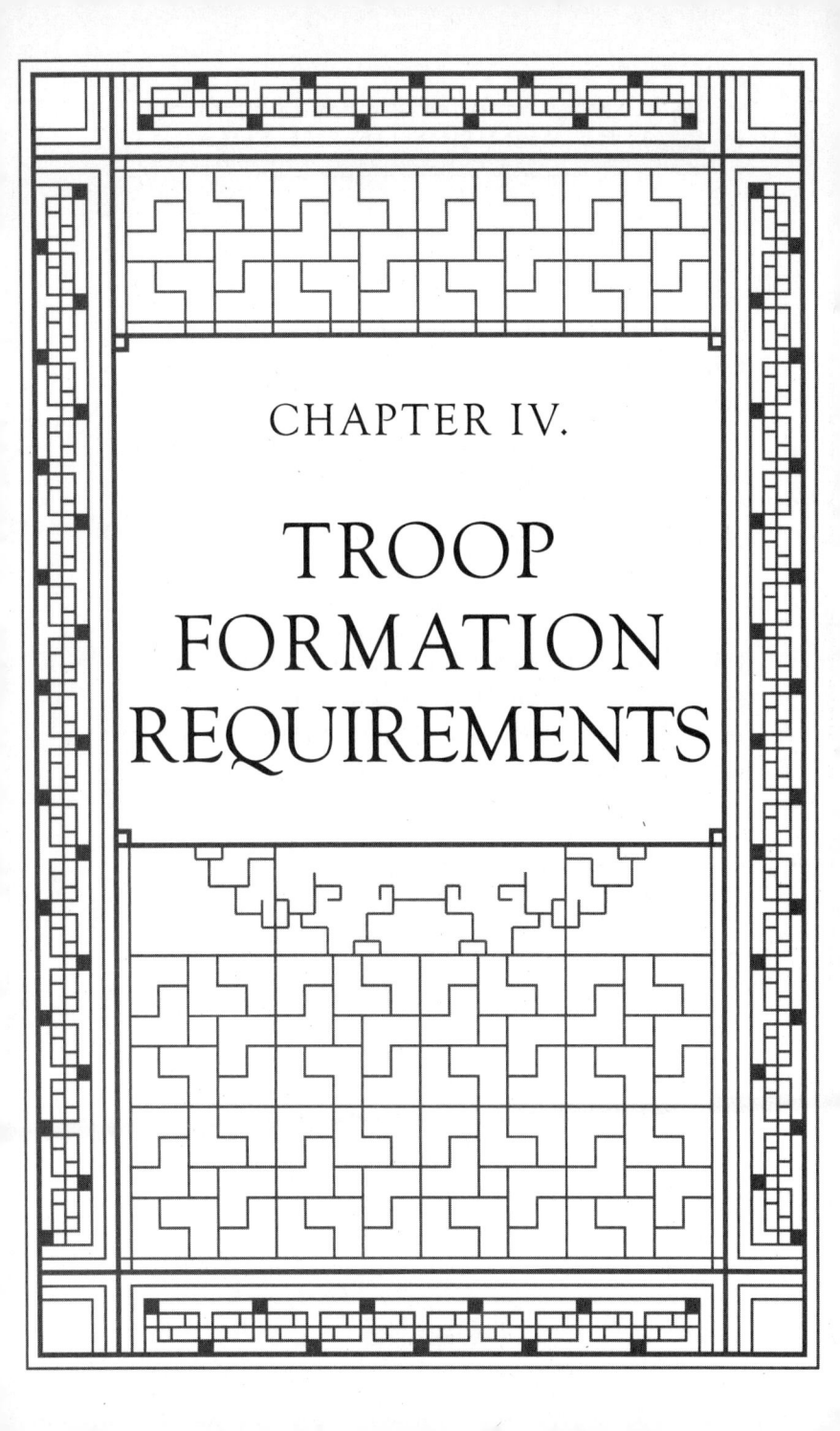

TROOP FORMATION REQUIREMENTS

THE METHODS OF THE SIMA

1

The principles of warfare are that positions should be strictly defined; administrative measures should be strictly adhered to; movement should be nimble; the soldiers' disposition should be calm; and the minds of the officers and people should be unified.

2

Rank and appoint men to office based on their morals and ability. Establish squads. Order the rows and files. Set the correct spacing between the horizontal and vertical formations. Investigate whether the orders are carried out.

3

Soldiers in standing formations should crouch down and advance; those who are in squatting formation should advance using their knees.

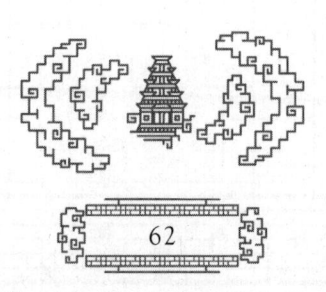

TROOP FORMATION REQUIREMENTS

4

If they are frightened, make the formation dense; if they are in danger, ask them to assume a sitting formation.

5

If you have a clear view of the enemy from a distance, you will not be frightened; if you have a clear view of the enemy near you, you will concentrate on the battle.

6

The position of soldiers in the formation is distributed according to left, right, row and column.

7

When not advancing, troops should take the sitting formation.

THE METHODS OF THE SIMA

8

When giving out orders, how troops should be positioned and how the weapons are carried in each formation's position should be taken into consideration.

9

If the chariots and horses are agitated and the soldiers are fearful, they should draw together so that the line is dense and use a kneeling or sitting formation, with the general going forward on his knees to calm them down with words of grace and admonition.

10

Have them get up, shout and advance using drums; signal a halt with the bells.

11

When the troops are resting, taking orders or having meals, ask them to sit down; and when there is a need to move, use knees to advance.

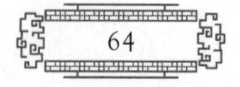

TROOP FORMATION REQUIREMENTS

12

On the battlefield, kill to stop soldiers from being hesitant, and shout at them to advance.

13

If they are too terrified of the enemy, do not threaten them with execution and severe punishment but display a magnanimity.

14

Speak to them about the way to survive and achieve accomplishment; supervise them in their duties to complete the tasks.

15

Within the Three Armies, all punishment has to be imposed within half a day; the injunctions given to individuals have to be enforced immediately, even without waiting for a meal.

THE METHODS OF THE SIMA

16

When the enemy are in doubts, such is an opportunity to subdue them.

17

In warfare, when the army is strong, it will last, and when the morale is strong, it will win.

18

If the camp is strong, it will last, and if the army is in danger, it will win.

19

When the soldiers sincerely seek battle, they will be firm, and when they are vigorous, they will win.

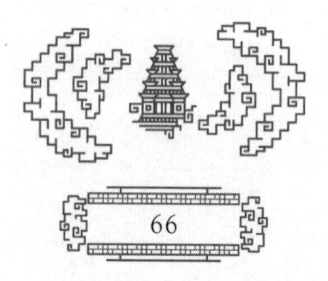

TROOP FORMATION REQUIREMENTS

20

With the armour, the army is secure; with weapons, the army attains victory.

21

Chariots are strengthened when they are dense, infantry are strengthened when they are in a seated formation, armour must be heavy to be strong, and weapons must be light and sharp to be victorious.

22

When soldiers have their mind set for victory, the next stage is to find out the situation of the enemy and see if there is a chance to attack.

23

When soldiers are filled with fear, the next stage is to find out what their fear is.

THE METHODS OF THE SIMA

24

Once feelings have been made clear, their consequences and causes should be treated the same. How the general handles both situations depends on his execution of authority.

25

In warfare, using small troops against enemy's troops is dangerous.

26

Using large troops against enemy's large troops does not guarantee victory.

27

Using small troops against enemy's large troops is asking for failure. Using large troops against small troops can achieve swift victory. Thus, war is also a comparison of strengths on both sides.

TROOP FORMATION REQUIREMENTS

28

When in encampment, be careful about the weapons and armours. When on the move, be cautious about the rows and files. When in battle, be careful about when to advance or stop.

29

In warfare, prudence will serve the purpose, and leading by example will convince the army.

30

If a general is impatient and disturbed, he will act rashly; if a general is calm and unhurried, he will be respectful in his dealings.

31

A tight drumbeat is a call to advance rapidly, a slow drumbeat is a call to advance slowly.

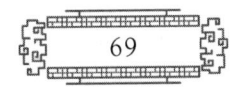

THE METHODS OF THE SIMA

32

When the uniforms are light, troops will feel agile. When the uniforms are heavy, troops will feel stalwart.

33

When the horses and chariots are sturdy, the armour and weapons are strong, then even a small force can function like a big one.

34

A general who likes to go along with the crowd will not achieve anything.

35

A general who always insists on his own decisions will see a lot of his troops sacrificed.

TROOP FORMATION REQUIREMENTS

36

A general who is scared of death and not courageous will leave his troops in doubts.

37

A general who fights without employing strategies will not achieve victories.

38

People will die out of love and gratitude, anger, fear, awe authority, righteousness or greed.

39

Thus in warfare, restraining people by decree can only make them afraid to die; moving people by moral righteousness can make them willing to die for justice.

THE METHODS OF THE SIMA

40

In warfare, either victory or defeat depends on whether or not it is in accordance with the time of day and the hearts of the people.

41

In warfare, the all Three Armies should not be on alert for more than three days, a small force of soldiers should not be on vigilant for more than half a day, and the order given to individuals should be fulfilled immediately.

42

The best way to conduct warfare is to win by strategy, and only secondarily by offensive warfare.

43

It is important to grasp the overall situation as well as the specific aspects in order to decide whether to win by strategy or by offensive warfare. And this is a question that should be weighed in war.

TROOP FORMATION REQUIREMENTS

44

All victories are only achieved when the whole Three Armies are united as one.

45

For drums, there are drums that direct the deployment of flags and pennants; drums for advancing the chariots, for war horses, for directing infantry, for taking over, for organizing or forming formations, and for standing and sitting. All seven should be prepared.

46

Whenever you are in battle, you should not hold too much weight if you are strong in battle.

47

Even if you have a strong army, do not use up all your strength at once when attacking, for it will endanger yourself.

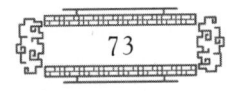

THE METHODS OF THE SIMA

48

In warfare, it is not the battle formations that are difficult, it is the fact that soldiers can be ordered into a formation fast that is difficult.

49

It is not the fact that soldiers can be ordered into a formation fast that is difficult, it is the ability of them to exercise flexibility in using formation that is difficult.

50

All in all, it is not the knowledge of formation that is difficult, it is the appropriate implementation of the formation that is difficult.

51

All men have their own personalities and they differ from region to region.

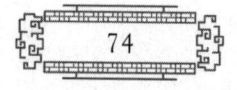

TROOP FORMATION REQUIREMENTS

52

Through teaching, these personalities can become customs. Customs differ from region to region. Through moral teaching, these customs can come together.

53

Just as one is not arrogant when losing a battle, one must not be arrogant when winning a battle, regardless of the size of the army.

54

Anyone who does not seek sharpness in weapons, toughness in armour, strength in vehicles, good horses, or efforts to increase the number of soldiers, has not mastered the art of winning battles.

55

Whenever a battle is fought, the glory is to be shared with the people when victory is won.

THE METHODS OF THE SIMA

56

If another battle is to be fought, the rewards and punishments are to be emphasised.

57

If you fail to achieve victory, accept the blame yourself. If you fight again, assume a leading position and do not repeat the tactics used last time.

58

Whether you win or not, do not deviate from this principle for it is the true principle.

59

Treat your soldiers with kindness and love to save them from distress, with morality to encourage them to fight, with wisdom to discern their merits and demerits, with bravery to lead them into battle, and with authority to make them obey orders.

TROOP FORMATION REQUIREMENTS

60

Reward them for their service with wealth, and inspire them to victory with merit.

61

Your thoughts shall be kind, your actions be moral and your conduct be wise.

62

You shall subdue your enemies with bravery, and let your integrity win hearts and minds for a long time.

63

By being humble and amiable, and by being harmonious with one another, by taking the blame for one's mistakes and giving the honour to others, one will be able to convince the soldiers and make them happy to serve.

THE METHODS OF THE SIMA

64

In warfare, attack the weak and quiet, avoid the strong and quiet. Attack the tired, avoid the well-trained. Attack those who are very afraid, avoid those who are alert. These have been the rules governing the army since antiquity.

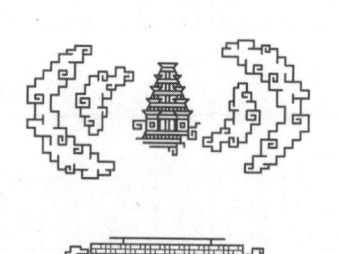

CHAPTER V.

EMPLOYING MASSES

THE METHODS OF THE SIMA

1

In warfare, when you employ a small number of people, their defence should be solid.

2

When you employ a large mass, they must be well-ordered.

3

With a small force it is advantageous to win using unorthodox methods; with a large mass, it is advantageous to use orthodox tactics.

4

When employing a large mass, they must be able to advance and stop; when employing a small number, they must be able to advance and withdraw.

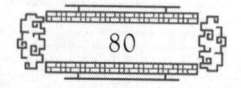

EMPLOYING MASSES

5

If you are fighting a weak enemy with a superior force, you should surround them from a distance and leave a gap to let them flee or attack them in turn in groups.

6

If you are fighting a superior enemy with a weaker force, you should bluff and confuse the enemy and use unexpected methods to gain victory.

7

If you are attacking an enemy that is occupying a strategic position, abandon your flags as if in flight.

8

And when the enemy attacks, turn around to mount a counter-attack.

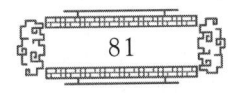

THE METHODS OF THE SIMA

9

If the enemy is heavily outnumbered, be aware of the situation and be prepared to fight under siege.

10

If the enemy is fewer and fearful, avoid them at the moment and attack when opportunity arises.

11

Whenever you are fighting, you should keep your back to the wind and lean on the high ground, rely on the high ground on your right and the danger on your left, pass swampy and crumbling ground quickly, and choose terrain with danger on all sides and high ground in the middle for camping.

12

In warfare, first set up a position and do not rush into battle.

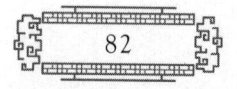

EMPLOYING MASSES

13

See how the enemy acts, then take action accordingly.

14

If the enemy has prepared a trap and is waiting for you to fall for it, hold off on attacking.

15

Do not drum to signal the advance, but await the moment when their masses arise.

16

If they attack, concentrate your forces and attack his weakness.

17

In warfare, use more or less of your forces to test the enemy to see how they changes.

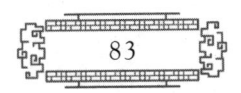

THE METHODS OF THE SIMA

18

Use sudden advances and retreats to see if the enemy's position is firm; approach and threaten the enemy to see if they are afraid; hold your troops still to see if they are slack; make a feint to see if they are suspicious; intercept them suddenly to see if his formation is in order.

19

Mount a strike when they are in doubt. Attack when they are unprepared so they are not able to fight with full strength.

20

Attack their well-ordered formation to disrupt their deployment.

21

Take advantage of the enemy's mistake of adventuring and advancing lightly.

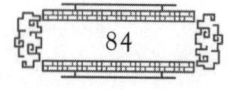

EMPLOYING MASSES

22

Prevent them from executing their strategies. Forcing them to abandon strategies. Destroy them when they are in fear.

23

Whenever you pursue a routed enemy, you must not stop, and if they stop all of a sudden, you must consider their intentions carefully.

24

Whenever you approach the enemy's headquarters, have a route of attack. When you are about to withdraw, ponder the retreat route.

25

In warfare, if you move too early, you will be exhausted easily; if you move too late, the soldiers maybe afraid.

THE METHODS OF THE SIMA

26

If you only pay attention to rest, you make your troops slack; if you don't rest at all, you are bound to make your troops tired; but if you rest for a long time, you will become war-weary.

27

Writing letters to families should be forbidden to stop soldiers from being homesick.

28

Selecting the best and equipping them with weapons to increase the strength of troops.

29

Abandoning armour and carrying minimal rations of food to motivate the troops.

EMPLOYING MASSES

30

From antiquity, this has been the administration of the army.

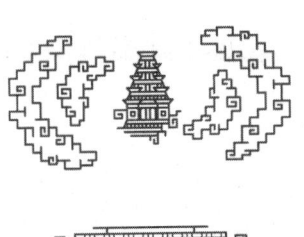